Classics

Classics

B Bounty
Books

First published in Great Britain in 1999 by
Hamlyn, a division of Octopus Publishing
Group Ltd

This edition published in 2008 by Bounty Books, a
division of Octopus Publishing Group Ltd
2–4 Heron Quays, London E14 4JP
Reprinted 2008
An Hachette Livre UK Company

ISBN: 978-0-753716-55-7

A CIP catalogue record for this book is available
from the British Library

Printed and bound in China

Notes

1 Standard level spoon measurements are
used in all recipes.

1 tablespoon = one 15 ml spoon
1 teaspoon = one 5 ml spoon

2 Both imperial and metric measurements
have been given in all recipes. Use one set of
measurements only and not a mixture of both.

3 Measurements for canned food have been
given as a standard metric equivalent.

4 Eggs should be medium unless otherwise
stated. The Department of Health advises that
eggs should not be consumed raw. This book
may contain dishes made with lightly cooked
eggs. It is prudent for more vulnerable people,
such as pregnant and nursing mothers,
invalids, the elderly, babies and young
children, to avoid uncooked or lightly cooked
dishes made with eggs. Once prepared, these
dishes should be used immediately.

5 Milk should be full fat unless otherwise
stated.

6 Poultry should be cooked thoroughly.
To test if poultry is cooked, pierce the flesh
through the thickest part with a skewer or
fork – the juices should run clear, never pink
or red.

7 Fresh herbs should be used unless
otherwise stated. If unavailable, use dried
herbs as an alternative but halve the
quantities stated.

8 Pepper should be freshly ground black
pepper unless otherwise stated; season
according to taste.

9 Ovens should be preheated to the specified
temperature – if using a fan-assisted oven,
follow the manufacturer's instructions for
adjusting the time and the temperature.

10 Do not re-freeze a dish that has been
frozen previously.

11 This book includes dishes made with nuts
and nut derivatives. It is advisable for
customers with known allergic reactions to
nuts and nut derivatives and those who may
be potentially vulnerable to these allergies,
such as pregnant and nursing mothers,
invalids, the elderly, babies and children, to
avoid dishes made with nuts and nut oils.
It is also prudent to check the labels of pre-
prepared ingredients for the possible inclusion
of nut derivatives.

12 Vegetarians should look for the 'V' symbol
on a cheese to ensure it is made with
vegetarian rennet. There are vegetarian forms
of Parmesan, feta, Cheddar, Cheshire, red
Leicester, dolcelatte and many goats' cheeses,
among others.

Whether they are served to start a
meal, as a light lunch or late-night
snack, these tempting dishes will
always be welcome.

Rich, slow-baked casseroles and
traditional pies, Braised Ham and Toad
in the Hole – classic meat dishes are
perfect for special occasions and
family meals alike.

From old favourites such as Roast
Turkey and traditional Chicken Pie, to
more exotic dishes like Kashmiri
Chicken and Crispy Orange Duck, this
section features a mouth-watering
array of succulent main courses.

Fish and shellfish bring a touch of
luxury to the table on any occasion,
from a simple midweek supper of Tuna
Fish Cakes to a celebratory meal of
Lobster Thermidor – enjoy!

Everyone loves the classic desserts,
such as Old English Trifle and Treacle
Pudding, and what teatime would be
complete without Shortbread and
Bakewell Tart?

contents

6

introduction

Classic recipes are those that are used by generations of cooks, again and again, despite changing fashions and fads in food and diet. These are the dishes cooked most often, and for good reason. Originally making use of home-grown and home-produced foods, but now incorporating exotic ingredients and different cooking styles as the nation's horizons have widened over the centuries, these are recipes that have stood the test of time and reflect our social history. For example, Kedgeree became a popular Anglo-Indian dish during the days of the Raj, but has stayed popular ever since even though few people today would recognise its origins. With such wide-ranging influences, classic dishes can be both comforting in their familiarity and exciting in their variety.

Unlike most other countries in the world, Britain draws its classic dishes from a wide range of other cuisines, and this book brings them together in one volume. The wealth of national dishes, some of which have survived for generations, are truly a part of British heritage. As well as a good choice of favourite recipes which originated in the British Isles, such as Chicken Pie, Lancashire Hot Pot and Sussex Pond Pudding, there are great national dishes from France (Coq au Vin and Cassoulet), Italy (Chunky Minestrone), Spain (Paella), India (Chicken Korma) and South America (Chilli Con Carne). There are excellent recipes covering all parts of a meal – starters, main courses and desserts – and there are delicious baking recipes and dishes suitable for snacks, light lunches and late suppers.

Meal Planning
Despite the wide variety of cultures and societies these recipes come from, they can work together surprisingly well, making meal planning from this book a lot of fun. Although there are noticeable differences between the way a chicken dish from France, say, is prepared and one from India – compare the delicate flavourings of a Chicken Véronique with a more heavily spiced but still creamily light Kashmiri Chicken, for instance – they both have in common a good understanding of how to turn a selection of basic ingredients into dishes that both satisfy the appetite and please the senses.

So, there is no need to be afraid of mixing dishes from different regional styles. A fresh Lemon and Avocado Soup can make a fine lead into a substantial main course dish like Carbonnade of Beef or a lighter but more highly spiced dish such as Lamb Tagine. However, an important point to remember when mixing and matching recipes is not to choose dishes so widely different in taste that one will swamp the other.

Getting the Best Out of Ingredients
All the recipes in this book were developed to make the best possible use of locally grown and produced foods – the better the quality of the food, the more tasty and succulent the dishes made from them. Because food today is more mass-produced

'Please, sir, I want some more.'

Charles Dickens, *Oliver Twist*

than it was in our parents' or grandparents' time, we need to be more vigilant when buying food to ensure that we get the freshest and best quality available whenever possible. Ingredients used in the recipes here that should be bought with extra care include eggs, which should always be free range, and fresh fish which must also be chosen carefully. Buy it the day it is to be cooked and look for a plump, firm, shiny and moist body, and a bright, fresh eye that has not sunk into the head. If the fish has too strong and fishy a smell, it is not very fresh. Take care also when selecting smoked haddock – it should always be properly smoked, and not dyed a vivid yellow as this suggests that many additives have been used in its production. Good-quality fish can be bought in most large supermarkets.

It is useful to bear in mind that well-hung beef has a better flavour than beef that is very fresh or has not been hung: look for lean that is a dark red colour and fat that is creamy and is visible in small flecks throughout the lean.

Vegetables should always be the freshest possible, with organically-grown vegetables having the added bonus of excellent flavour. Always try to prepare vegetables just before they are to be used, as soaking loses valuable vitamins and minerals and leaving vegetables lying about causes them to lose their fresh crispness. Root vegetables, if young and fresh, may not need peeling, but just a good scrub. For vegetables that do need peeling, use a vegetable peeler rather than a kitchen knife to shave off as fine a layer of skin as possible.

Unless they are to be used immediately, it is best not to wash mushrooms. Simply wipe off any of the growing medium that may be clinging to them with kitchen paper. Most mushrooms do not need to be peeled.

When choosing stocks at the supermarket, chose bouillon cubes or fresh or frozen stocks, rather than stock cubes, which tend to be over salty and also contain quite high amounts of fat.

Classic Extras

Just as there are many classic recipes, so there are many classic combinations of ingredients or specially prepared ingredients used in cooking. Among those which may be used with recipes in this book are:

Beurre manié – equal amounts of plain flour and softened butter are worked together into a paste and stirred into stews and sauces to thicken them.

Bouquet garni – a bunch of fresh herbs tied together and used to flavour soups, stews and casseroles; it is removed from the cooked dish before serving. A basic bouquet garni combination is sprigs of fresh parsley and thyme and a bay leaf. Fresh marjoram, a piece of celery and other herbs may be used, too.

Clarified butter – salted butter turned into a clear yellow liquid which can be heated to a higher temperature than butter during cooking, without burning. Melt the salted butter over gentle heat and cook it, without stirring, until it foams. Keep cooking the butter gently until it stops foaming, then set it aside to let the milky solids sink to the bottom of the pan. Strain the liquid through muslin and discard the milky solids.

Vinaigrette – a mixture of oil and vinegar, seasoned with salt and pepper, sometimes flavoured with herbs and used to dress salads or vegetables. The classic mixture is 3 or 4 parts of oil to 1 part of vinegar, and the classic combination is olive oil and wine vinegar.

Chantilly cream – thick cream whipped to soft peaks and flavoured with a little caster sugar and 2 or 3 drops of vanilla extract. Serve with hot or cold desserts.

Crumble topping – an all-time favourite hot fruit pudding. The basic crumble mixture is 6 parts flour, 3 parts butter or margarine and 2 parts sugar. Mix the flour and sugar together and rub in the butter in small pieces until the mixture resembles breadcrumbs. Spoon the mixture over prepared fresh fruit sprinkled with a little water in a baking dish – apples, apricots, peaches and rhubarb are top choices. Sprinkle demerara sugar over the crumble topping and bake in a preheated oven at 190°C (375°F), Gas Mark 5, for about 25 minutes.

Fruit fool – another delicious fruit dessert made by whipping thick cream to soft peaks and lightly mixing it with sweetened puréed fruit. Try for a marbled effect so that the colour of the fruit shows in the cream.

Healthy Classic Cooking

Many classic recipes seem less than healthy to today's cooks. Although a certain amount of fat is essential in a healthy diet, much of it can be reduced or eliminated, and many of the recipes in this book have been so adapted. You will find vegetable oil being used instead of lard or butter, for instance, while cooking methods have also been adapted to cut down on the amount of fat used in the original recipes.

Where once butter and cream were essential, it is now possible to replace them with low-fat dairy products. Yogurt makes a good substitute for cream in creamy sauces, though it is essential not to allow the sauce to boil once the yogurt has been added, or it may curdle. Fromage frais and crème fraîche make excellent and delicious low-fat replacements for cream in desserts.

soups, starters & snacks

500 g (1 lb) yellow onions, peeled

50 g (2 oz) butter or margarine

25 g (1 oz) plain flour

1.2 litres (2 pints) beef stock

1 tablespoon cognac (optional)

½ teaspoon Dijon mustard

salt and pepper

To Garnish:

6 slices French bread

75 g (3 oz) Gruyère cheese

Serves 6
Preparation time: 10 minutes
Cooking time: 40 minutes

1 Slice the onions into fairly thick even rings. Melt the butter or margarine in a saucepan. Add the onions and cook over a moderate heat, stirring constantly, until soft and pale gold in colour. Sprinkle in the flour, stir for about 1 minute, then gradually pour in the stock. Bring the mixture to the boil, stirring constantly. Add salt and pepper to taste.

2 Lower the heat and simmer for 20–25 minutes. Add the cognac, if using. Stir in the Dijon mustard. Keep the onion soup hot.

3 Grill the bread for the garnish until it is lightly browned. Sprinkle each slice with grated Gruyère cheese. Pour the soup into heatproof bowls and float a slice of cheese-topped bread on each portion. Put the bowls under a preheated grill until the cheese melts and bubbles. Serve immediately.

■ Traditional French onion soup uses beef stock. For a vegetarian alternative, use vegetable stock. The vegetable stock could be made richer by boiling it for 10 minutes with 125 g (4 oz) chopped open cap mushrooms. Strain the stock and use according to the recipe.

french onion soup

chunky minestrone

1 Heat the oil and bacon rinds in a large pan. Add the onions, garlic and diced bacon and cook gently for 5 minutes. Remove the bacon rinds. Add the chicken stock and bring to the boil. Add the tomatoes and carrots. Cover the pan and cook steadily for 15 minutes, adding a little seasoning, if necessary. At the end of this time, check there is sufficient liquid left to cook the cabbage and pasta. If not, add a little more stock or water and bring back to the boil.

2 Add the cabbage, pasta and petit pois. Cook for 15 minutes or until the pasta is tender. Add the canned beans and heat for a few minutes.

3 Serve the soup topped with the grated cheese and herbs.

2 tablespoons olive oil

2 bacon rashers, derinded and diced (rinds reserved)

2 onions, finely chopped

2 garlic cloves, finely chopped

600 ml (1 pint) chicken stock

2 large tomatoes, skinned and chopped

2 carrots, finely grated

75 g (3 oz) white cabbage, finely shredded

50 g (2 oz) penne or macaroni

75 g (3 oz) frozen petit pois

250 g (8 oz) canned baked beans in tomato sauce

salt and pepper

Topping:

grated Parmesan cheese

chopped basil and thyme

Serves 4	
Preparation time: 15 minutes	
Cooking time: 40–45 minutes	

lemon & avocado soup

1 Halve the avocados, remove the stones and the peel. Either mash the avocado flesh with the lemon zest and juice or liquidize it with all the ingredients. Adjust the amount of lemon juice according to taste.

2 If mashing the avocado, gradually add the stock and cream, or yogurt or fromage frais, beating briskly to give a smooth texture.

3 Chill the soup and add the garnish just before serving.

■ To prevent the avocados turning brown, do not prepare them until you have all of the ingredients to hand. To give a spicier flavour, add a few drops of Tabasco sauce or a pinch of cayenne pepper.

2 medium avocados

1–2 teaspoons finely grated lemon zest

2–3 tablespoons lemon juice

450 ml (¾ pint) vegetable or chicken stock

150 ml (¼ pint) single cream, natural yogurt, or fromage frais

salt and pepper

To Garnish:

finely chopped spring onions

diced tomato (optional)

Serves 4

Preparation time: 10 minutes

scotch broth

1 Put the lamb, 3 onions, 3 turnips and 2 carrots into a large pan with the water, salt and peppercorns. Bring to the boil, cover and simmer for 3 hours. Allow to get quite cold and then remove all the fat. Pour off the stock and reserve. Take the meat off the bones, discarding the fat and vegetables.

2 Wash out the pan to remove any traces of fat, then return the stock to it, with the remaining onions, turnips and carrot, the leek, celery and pearl barley. Cover and simmer for about 40 minutes.

3 Cut the lamb into small pieces, add to the broth and boil for another 5 minutes until the meat has warmed through. Serve hot.

1 kg (2 lb) breast of lamb or scrag end of neck

5 onions, finely sliced

5 turnips, finely sliced

3 large carrots, finely sliced

1.8 litres (3 pints) water

1 teaspoon salt

12 peppercorns

1 leek, finely sliced

2 celery sticks, finely sliced

3 tablespoons pearl barley

Serves 6

Preparation time: 20 minutes, plus cooling

Cooking time: 3¾ hours

omelette arnold bennett

1 Mix the smoked haddock with the Parmesan. Season with pepper to taste. Melt the butter in a heavy frying or omelette pan and swirl the pan until it is completely coated with butter. Do not allow the butter to brown.

2 Pour in the eggs which should sizzle slightly, then with either a spatula or small fish slice, move the eggs into the middle but tip the pan so that the uncooked egg which is left runs over and covers the bottom.

3 When the bottom is just set but the top is still creamy, spoon over the fish and cheese mixture evenly. Pour the cream smoothly on top. Remove the omelette pan from the heat, sprinkle the top with freshly ground pepper and put under a preheated hot grill until it is puffed up and golden.

4 It is not necessary to fold this omelette; simply slide it off the pan, cream side up, on to a hot plate and serve.

300 g (10 oz) smoked haddock, cooked, skinned and flaked

2 tablespoons grated Parmesan cheese

1 teaspoon butter

6 eggs, lightly beaten

3–4 tablespoons double or whipping cream

pepper

Serves 2

Preparation time: 15 minutes

Cooking time: 7 minutes

■ This snack or late supper dish was created by a chef at the Savoy Hotel for the writer Arnold Bennett when he worked in London as a theatre critic.

kedgeree

1 Cook the rice in boiling salted water for about 12 minutes, or according to packet instructions, until each grain is dry and fluffy, then set aside and keep warm.

2 Poach the haddock in a little water for 10 minutes, drain and break the fish into large flakes. Meanwhile, hardboil the eggs, shell them, then cut half an egg into wedges for the garnish; chop the rest.

3 Heat the butter or margarine in a large pan and fry the leek for 3 minutes until soft but not coloured. Add the fish, cooked rice and just enough cream to moisten. Heat gently, stirring carefully, so the flakes of fish are not broken. Add the chopped egg to the mixture and season to taste. Spoon the mixture on to warmed serving dishes and garnish with the reserved egg wedges and some finely chopped parsley.

125 g (4 oz) long-grain rice

500 g (1 lb) smoked haddock

2 eggs

50 g (2 oz) butter or margarine

1 leek, finely chopped

2–3 tablespoons single cream

salt and pepper

finely chopped parsley, to garnish

Serves 4

Preparation time: 10 minutes

Cooking time: 30 minutes

■ This Anglo-Indian dish originates from the era of the British Raj. It is a very good and filling breakfast or brunch dish. If time is short, cook the rice, eggs and haddock in advance and assemble the dish (step 3) just before serving, making sure the ingredients are piping hot.

cornish pasties

1 For the pastry, sift the salt and flour into a bowl, then rub in the fat with the fingers until the mixture resembles coarse breadcrumbs. Gradually add enough iced water to make a stiff dough, kneading lightly with your hands until it is smooth. Wrap in clingfilm and chill for at least 30 minutes. For the filling, mix the meat and vegetables together with the water and season very well.

2 Roll out the pastry on a floured surface to about 5 mm (¼ inch) thick and cut into 4 circles about 20 cm (8 inches) in diameter. Divide the mixture between the 4 circles, filling only one half of the circle. Dampen the edges with cold water, fold over to cover the mixture and press the edges together with a fork or the fingers. Alternatively, put the filling in the middle of the pastry circle and draw up the edges to the centre top.

3 Brush the pasties with milk or a little beaten egg, and make a small slit on top. Put them on a greased baking sheet and bake in a preheated oven, 220°C (425°F), Gas Mark 7, for 15 minutes, then reduce the oven temperature to 180°C (350°F), Gas Mark 4, and bake for 35–40 minutes more. Serve the pasties hot or cold.

Pastry:

¼ teaspoon salt

500 g (1 lb) plain flour

250 g (8 oz) butter

6 tablespoons iced water

Filling:

500 g (1 lb) finely chopped lean beef or lamb

250 g (8 oz) potatoes, coarsely grated

1 small piece of turnip or swede, coarsely grated

3–4 tablespoons cold water

a little milk or egg, to glaze

salt and pepper

Serves 4

Preparation time: 1 hour, plus chilling

Cooking time: 50–55 minutes

■ In a traditional Cornish pastry, the meat is finely chopped, not minced, and the vegetables are grated.

irish smoked salmon with scrambled eggs

1 Melt the butter in a saucepan until foaming. Place the eggs in a bowl and mix well with a fork. Add the milk and season to taste.

2 Pour the eggs into the foaming butter. Stir with a wooden spoon over a gentle heat, scraping the bottom of the pan and bringing the outside edges to the middle. The eggs are cooked when they form soft creamy curds and are barely set.

3 Remove from the heat, stir in the cream, if using, the salmon and the chives or dill and pile onto the hot brown toast on a warmed serving plate. Serve immediately.

15 g (½ oz) butter

3 large eggs

1 tablespoon milk

1 tablespoon cream (optional)

50 g (2 oz) smoked salmon, cut into narrow strips

1 teaspoon finely snipped chives or dill

1–2 slices warm wheaten bread, toasted and buttered

salt and pepper

Serves 1
Preparation time: 5 minutes
Cooking time: 3–4 minutes

parma ham & lemon

1 Arrange the ham in swathes on plates with the lemon halves. Season to taste with pepper and serve with buttered wholemeal toast.

■ Alternatively, serve the Parma ham with melon. Cut 1 sweet, ripe melon, such as Charentais or Ogen, into quarters. Drape the slices of ham over and sprinkle with black pepper.

150–200 g (5–7 oz) Parma ham

1 lemon, halved and each half wrapped in a piece of clean muslin (optional)

crushed black peppercorns

buttered wholemeal toast, to serve

Serves 2

Preparation time: 5 minutes

1 large onion

1 garlic clove

500 g (1 lb) belly pork

small glass of port

1 teaspoon mint, chopped

250 g (8 oz) lamb's liver, finely chopped

3 rindless streaky bacon rashers, finely chopped

50 g (2 oz) mushrooms, finely chopped

1 egg, beaten

salt and pepper

rosemary sprigs, to garnish

1 Put the onion, garlic and pork into a food processor and work until smooth. Turn into a bowl, stir in the port and mint and season to taste. Cover closely and leave to marinate in the refrigerator overnight.

2 Mix the liver, bacon and mushrooms into the port mixture. Stir in the egg. Spoon into a foil-lined 500 g (1 lb) loaf tin and bake in a preheated oven, 180°C (350°F), Gas Mark 4, for 1½ hours. Carefully pour off the fat and leave to cool.

3 To serve, remove the pâté from the tin, place on a serving dish and garnish with sprigs of rosemary.

Serves 8
Preparation time: 10–15 minutes, plus marinating and cooling
Cooking time: 1½ hours

pork & port pâté

1 Place the flour in a bowl. Add the butter and rub in with the fingertips until the mixture resembles fine breadcrumbs. Add the egg yolk and enough cold water to mix to a firm dough. Cover and chill for 30 minutes.

2 Roll out the dough on a lightly floured surface and use to line a 23 cm (9 inch) flan tin. Chill the pastry case for 30 minutes. Fill with crumpled foil and bake in a preheated oven, 200°C (400°F), Gas Mark 6, for 15 minutes. Remove the foil and bake for a further 10 minutes. Take the pastry case out of the oven and lower the oven temperature to 180°C (350°F), Gas Mark 4.

3 Meanwhile, make the filling. Grill the bacon until crisp, then drain it on kitchen paper; crumble or cut the cooled bacon into pieces. Beat the cream and eggs in a bowl with the nutmeg and salt and pepper to taste. Sprinkle the bacon over the flan case and pour the cream and egg filling over the top.

4 Place the flan tin on a baking sheet and bake for about 30–35 minutes, until the filling is just set and the pastry is golden brown. Serve the quiche warm or cold.

quiche lorraine

Pastry:

175 g (6 oz) plain flour

75 g (3 oz) chilled butter, diced

1 egg yolk, beaten

1–2 tablespoons cold water

Filling:

175 g (6 oz) rindless smoked back bacon

250 ml (8 fl oz) single cream

2 eggs, beaten

pinch of grated nutmeg

salt and pepper

Serves 4–6

Preparation time: 20 minutes, plus chilling

Cooking time: 55–1 hour

leek &
potato bake

1 Place the potatoes in a saucepan of salted boiling water and parboil for 3 minutes. Drain and slice.

2 Place the leeks in a greased ovenproof dish and season to taste with pepper. Arrange the potatoes on the top and pour the cream over. Cover with foil and bake in a preheated oven, 190°C (375°F), Gas Mark 5, for about 45 minutes until the potatoes are tender.

3 Sprinkle with the cheese and breadcrumbs and cook under a preheated moderate grill until the top is browned. Serve at once.

1.25 kg (2½ lb) potatoes, peeled

500 g (1 lb) leeks, trimmed and sliced

150 ml (¼ pint) single cream

50 g (2 oz) Cheddar cheese, grated

25 g (1 oz) fresh breadcrumbs

salt and pepper

Serves 6
Preparation time: 20 minutes
Cooking time: 50 minutes

■ This makes a great brunch or late supper dish. It can be placed in the oven, on the timer while you are out, to be browned under the grill on your return.

classic hamburgers ●

crusty shepherd's pie ●

barbecued italian sausages with mushrooms ●

farmhouse bake ●

beef & guinness pie ●

chilli con carne ●

toad in the hole ●

carbonnade of beef ●

beef cobbler ●

goulash ●

braised ham ●

cassoulet ●

lancashire hot pots ●

steak & kidney pie ●

lamb tagine ●

lamb dhansak ●

meat dishes

28

classic
hamburgers

1 In a large bowl, combine the minced meat, Worcestershire sauce, grated onion and breadcrumbs. Season to taste and mix well. Form the mixture into 6 round flat cakes.

2 Heat a large frying pan. If the meat is very lean, you may need to lightly oil the pan. Fry the burgers for 2–3 minutes on each side. Depending on how thick they are, you may need to cook them a bit longer, according to personal taste.

3 Serve on toasted hamburger buns or large rolls with onion rings, tomato slices, salad leaves or your choice of toppings.

500 g (1lb) best-quality chuck steak, minced

3 tablespoons Worcestershire sauce

50 g (2 oz) grated onion

50 g (2 oz) soft fresh breadcrumbs

oil, for frying

salt and pepper

To Garnish:

sesame seed rolls or hamburger buns, toasted

onion rings

tomato slices

salad leaves

Makes 6
Preparation time: 10 minutes
Cooking time: 4–6 minutes

crusty shepherd's pie

1 Heat the oil in a frying pan, add the bacon and onion and fry for 5 minutes, until softened. Add the lamb and fry, stirring, until evenly browned. Stir in the herbs, wine and passata and season. Bring to the boil, then lower the heat and simmer, uncovered, for 25 minutes, until the lamb is tender and the sauce thickened.

2 To make the scone topping, put the flour in a bowl with salt and pepper to taste. Rub in the diced butter until the mixture resembles fine breadcrumbs. Stir in the mustard and 50 g (2 oz) of the cheese, then add enough milk to make a soft dough.

3 Knead the dough briefly on a lightly floured surface, then roll out to a thickness of 1 cm (½ inch). Stamp into 5 cm (2 inch) scones. Reroll the trimmings and stamp out more rounds. Transfer the meat mixture to a greased 1.2 litre (2 pint) pie dish. Arrange the scones over the top, brush with milk and sprinkle with the remaining cheese. Bake in a preheated oven, 200°C (400°F), Gas Mark 6, for about 25 minutes, until the topping is golden brown. Serve hot.

■ Passata is an Italian preparation of sieved plum tomatoes. The thick purée is available in bottles or cans from most supermarkets and delicatessens.

1 tablespoon olive oil

4 rindless smoked streaky bacon rashers, chopped

1 onion, chopped

500 g (1 lb) minced lamb

1 teaspoon dried oregano

2 tablespoons chopped parsley

150 ml (¼ pint) red wine

425 g (14 oz) passata

salt and pepper

Scone Topping:

250 g (8 oz) self-raising flour

50 g (2 oz) chilled butter, diced

2 teaspoons wholegrain mustard

75 g (3 oz) mature Cheddar cheese, grated

125 ml (4 fl oz) milk

Serves 4–6
Preparation time: 20 minutes
Cooking time: 55 minutes

barbecued italian sausages with mushrooms

1 To make the polenta, bring the measured water and salt to the boil in a large saucepan. Reduce the heat slightly, and add the polenta in a thin stream, beating all the time. Cook, stirring constantly, for 20–30 minutes, until the mixture comes away from the sides of the pan. Tip the polenta on to a board or baking sheet. Leave to cool. Cut into thick slices, brush with olive oil and set aside.

2 To prepare the mushrooms, remove the stalks and brush the caps all over with the reserved oil from the tomatoes. Finely chop the stalks and place in a bowl with the chopped sun-dried tomatoes, cheese and pine nuts. Add salt and pepper to taste and mix to combine. Stuff the mushroom caps with this mixture.

3 Place 2 stuffed mushrooms on a piece of foil large enough to enclose them, bring up the edges and seal well. Repeat with the remaining mushrooms.

4 Cook the sausages, polenta slices and mushroom parcels on an oiled grill over hot barbecue coals for 15–20 minutes, or until the sausages are cooked, the mushrooms are tender and the polenta is lightly crisp on the outside. Serve at once.

8 large chestnut or medium field mushrooms

8 sun-dried tomato halves, chopped, with 4 tablespoons oil reserved

250 g (8 oz) Gorgonzola or dolcelatte cheese, crumbled

50 g (2 oz) pine nuts, toasted

8 Italian sausages or other good-quality sausages

Polenta:

750 ml (1¼ pints) water

1 teaspoon salt

250 g (8 oz) polenta (corn meal)

2 tablespoons olive oil

Serves 4

Preparation time: 20 minutes

Cooking time: 35–50 minutes

■ To toast pine nuts, dry fry them in a hot frying pan, stirring constantly, until they become a golden brown colour.

1 Melt half the butter in a pan and fry the bacon until cooked and beginning to brown. Remove from the pan and fry the onion and mushrooms until cooked and beginning to colour.

2 Cut the potatoes into wedges and arrange with the fried bacon, mushrooms and onions in an oval 750–900 ml (1¼–1½ pint) ovenproof dish. Season to taste and add the chopped parsley.

3 Pour over the cream and cover with the grated Cheddar. Bake in a preheated oven, 180°C (350°F), Gas Mark 4, for 20–30 minutes until crisp and golden on the top and very hot. Serve with grilled tomatoes, if liked.

50 g (2 oz) butter

8 smoked back bacon rashers, cut into strips

1 large onion, finely chopped

125 g (4 oz) mushrooms, sliced

6 potatoes, boiled

1 tablespoon chopped parsley

150 ml (¼ pint) double cream

125 g (4 oz) Cheddar cheese, grated

salt and pepper

Serves 4

Preparation time: 20 minutes

Cooking time: about 30–40 minutes

farmhouse bake

■ To make a pasta supper dish with the same rich, comforting flavours, substitute the potato wedges with 375 g (12 oz) dried macaroni or penne, boiled until just tender. Serve with a crisp green salad.

beef & guinness pie

1 Heat the oil in a large pan, add the beef and fry until browned. Add the onions and celery and fry for 5 minutes. Stir in the flour and cook for 1 minute. Gradually stir in the Guinness and stock until the liquid is thickened. Stir in the remaining ingredients and season. Cover the pan and cook for 1½ hours, until tender. Pour into a 1.5 litre (2½ pint) pie dish and allow to cool slightly. Remove the bay leaves.

2 To make the pastry, mix the flour with a little salt in a bowl. Stir in the walnuts and mustard seeds. Add the butter and rub in with your fingertips until the mixture resembles breadcrumbs. Stir in enough cold water, about 2–3 tablespoons, to make a firm dough. Turn out on to a floured surface and knead briefly. Roll out to 5 cm (2 inches) larger than the pie dish; cut off a strip 2.5 cm (1 inch) wide all round. Dampen the rim of the dish with water and press the pastry strip on top. Dampen the strip and cover with the pastry lid.

3 Decorate the pie by pinching the edges of the pastry between thumb and finger. Make a small hole in the centre to allow the steam to escape. Bake in a preheated oven, 190°C (375°F), Gas Mark 5, for 35–40 minutes, until crisp and golden brown.

2 tablespoons oil

1 kg (2 lb) lean braising steak, cubed

2 onions, thinly sliced

2 celery sticks, chopped

25 g (1 oz) plain flour

450 ml (¾ pint) Guinness

150 ml (¼ pint) beef stock

2 teaspoons light muscovado sugar

2 bay leaves

2 teaspoons Worcestershire sauce

1 tablespoon tomato purée

125 g (4 oz) stoned ready-to-eat prunes

salt and pepper

Pastry:

175 g (6 oz) plain flour

25 g (1 oz) walnuts, finely chopped

1 teaspoon mustard seeds

125 g (4 oz) chilled butter, diced

Serves 6

Preparation time: 25 minutes, plus chilling

Cooking time: 2–2¼ hours

chilli con carne

1 Put the drained beans into a pan of cold water, bring to the boil, boil rapidly for 10 minutes, then drain.

2 Heat the oil in a flameproof casserole, add the beef and cook, turning frequently, until browned. Add the onion and green chilli and cook for 2–3 minutes. Add the oregano, cumin, chilli flakes, tomatoes and their juice, stock and beans to the casserole and bring to the boil.

3 Cover the casserole and put it into a preheated oven, 160°C (325°F), Gas Mark 3. Cook for 1½ hours, or until the beef and beans are tender. Taste and adjust the seasoning if necessary, before serving.

175 g (6 oz) pinto beans, soaked overnight

2 tablespoons oil

625 g (1¼ lb) chuck steak, finely diced

1 onion, chopped

1 small green chilli, deseeded and chopped

1 teaspoon dried oregano

1 tablespoon ground cumin

½ teaspoon dried red chilli flakes

425 g (14 oz) canned chopped tomatoes

300 ml (½ pint) beef stock

salt and pepper

Serves 4

Preparation time: 15 minutes, plus soaking

Cooking time: 1¾ hours

250 g (8 oz) plain flour, sifted

1 teaspoon salt

2 large eggs, beaten

600 ml (1 pint) milk

4 tablespoons beef dripping

12 lightly grilled sausages

1 Put the flour and salt into a bowl and make a well in the centre. Add the beaten eggs and half the milk and mix to a smooth paste, beating for at least 5 minutes. Add the remaining milk and beat again, then thin with cold water to the consistency of thick cream. Leave the batter to stand for about 30 minutes.

Serves 6

Preparation time: 15 minutes, plus standing

Cooking time: 35–40 minutes

2 Heat the dripping and sausages in a baking tin or in 6 large separate Yorkshire pudding tins. The fat should be so hot that when the batter is poured in it sizzles. With your fingers, add a few drops of cold water to the batter and stir with a fork.

3 Pour the batter into the hot fat, then put immediately in a preheated oven, 220°C (425°F), Gas Mark 7, near the top. For the single pudding, cook for 35–40 minutes, for the smaller ones, 15–20 minutes. Do not open the oven door until the minimum cooking time has elapsed. The pudding is ready when the top is golden brown and crisp and the centre is cooked, but still creamy.

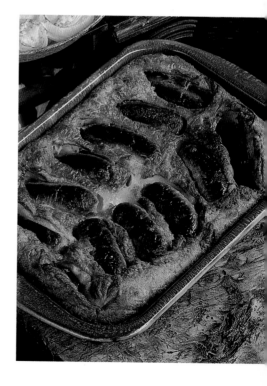

toad in the hole

carbonnade of beef

1 Toss the meat in seasoned flour until well coated. Reserve any remaining flour. Melt the butter and oil in a frying pan, add the bacon and fry gently until browned. Transfer to a casserole. Add the onions to the frying pan and fry gently; then add the meat and brown it on both sides. Transfer the onions and meat to the casserole.

2 Sprinkle the reserved flour into the pan, add the ale, stock and 1 teaspoon of the French mustard, and scrape the juices from the sides of the pan into the mixture. Stir together, season with salt and pepper, then pour over the meat in the casserole. Add the bouquet garni and parsley.

3 Put the covered casserole in a preheated oven, 180°C (350°F), Gas Mark 4, and cook for 1½ hours or until tender. Remove the bouquet garni, taste and adjust seasoning and consistency, if necessary. Place the slices of French bread, spread with the remaining mustard, on top of the meat and return the casserole, uncovered, to the oven for a further 15–20 minutes until the bread is golden brown. Serve at once.

750 g (1½ lb) braising steak, trimmed and cut into 5 cm (2 inch) slices

1 tablespoon plain flour, seasoned

50 g (2 oz) butter

1 tablespoon oil

50 g (2 oz) streaky bacon, derinded and diced

3 large onions, thinly sliced

300 ml (½ pint) brown ale

300 ml (½ pint) beef stock

5 teaspoons French mustard

1 bouquet garni

2 tablespoons chopped parsley

8 slices French bread

salt and pepper

Serves 4

Preparation time: 25 minutes

Cooking time: 1¾–2 hours

1 Heat 2 tablespoons of the oil in a flameproof casserole. Toss the meat in the flour and fry in the oil over a high heat until golden brown. Reduce the heat, add the remaining oil and the vegetables, and fry gently for a few minutes. Add the bay leaf, stock and salt and pepper to taste and bring to the boil. Cover the casserole, transfer it to a preheated oven, 180°C (350°F), Gas Mark 4, and cook for 1 hour.

2 Meanwhile, make the scone topping: sieve the flour and salt into a bowl, then rub in the fat until the mixture resembles fine breadcrumbs. Add the herbs and mix with the egg and milk to a soft dough. Roll out on a floured board to 1 cm (½ inch) thick and cut into rounds or small triangles.

3 Remove the casserole from the oven, taste and adjust the seasoning and remove the bay leaf. Increase the temperature to 220°C (425°F), Gas Mark 7, and arrange the scones on top of the meat. Return the casserole, uncovered, to the top of the oven for 15 minutes, or until the scone topping is golden brown.

4 tablespoons oil

500 g (1 lb) stewing steak, trimmed and cut into small cubes

1 tablespoon seasoned plain flour

2 onions, diced

2 carrots, diced

1 small turnip, diced

1 bay leaf

450 ml (¾ pint) beef stock

salt and pepper

Scone Topping:

125 g (4 oz) self-raising flour

¼ teaspoon salt

50 g (2 oz) butter or margarine

¼ teaspoon mixed herbs

1 egg

2 tablespoons milk

Serves 4
Preparation time: 30 minutes
Cooking time: 1½ hours

beef cobbler

1 Heat the oil in a frying pan and fry the meat until brown on all sides. Reduce the heat and sprinkle the paprika and flour over the meat, turning it to absorb the flour. After about 2–3 minutes pour the stock into the frying pan and stir gently. Pour the meat and stock into a casserole.

2 Rinse the pan, melt the butter in it and sweat the onions and carrots gently. Add the herbs, tomatoes, purée, lemon juice, diced potato and salt and pepper to taste.

3 Pour the tomato mixture over the meat in the casserole and cook, covered, in a preheated oven, 160°C (325°F), Gas Mark 3, for 1 hour. Add the onions and return for a further 45 minutes. Before serving the casserole, remove the bay leaf, taste and adjust the seasoning, stir in the soured cream and garnish with parsley.

2 tablespoons oil

500 g (1 lb) braising steak, trimmed and cubed

2 teaspoons paprika

2 teaspoons flour

300 ml (½ pint) stock

25 g (1 oz) butter

250 g (8 oz) onions, diced

250 g (8 oz) carrots, diced

1 bay leaf

good pinch of thyme

425 g (14 oz) canned tomatoes with their juice

1 tablespoon tomato purée

1 teaspoon lemon juice

1 potato, diced

8 small onions

1 tablespoon soured cream

salt and pepper

finely chopped parsley, to garnish

Serves 4
Preparation time: 10–15 minutes
Cooking time: 2 hours

goulash

braised ham

1 Soak the ham in cold water to cover for several hours. Drain, discarding the water. Place the ham in a casserole, pour in the pale ale, season with pepper and cook, covered, in a preheated oven, 180°C (350°F), Gas Mark 4 for 40 minutes.

2 Remove the ham from the casserole and discard half the ale. Cut away the skin from the ham and score the fat diagonally. Mix together the honey, sugar and dry mustard and rub over the ham. Stud cloves into the ham surface in a diamond pattern and return the ham and remaining ale to the casserole.

3 Increase the oven temperature to 200°C (400°F), Gas Mark 6, and cook the casserole, uncovered, for another 30 minutes, basting the joint every 10 minutes. Serve garnished with wedges of orange and watercress.

1 kg (2 lb) forelock or middle gammon

300 ml (½ pint) pale ale

2 tablespoons honey

4 tablespoons demerara sugar

1 teaspoon dry mustard

12 cloves

pepper

To Garnish:

orange wedges

watercress

Serves 4
Preparation time: 15 minutes, plus soaking
Cooking time: 1 hour 10 minutes

cassoulet

250 g (8 oz) dried white haricot beans, soaked overnight

750 ml (1¼ pints) beef stock

125 g (4 oz) fresh pork rind, diced

8 garlic cloves, peeled

1 carrot, trimmed and lightly scraped

1 onion, studded with 4 cloves

2 tablespoons oil

125 g (4 oz) lean pork, cubed

125 g (4 oz) salt pork, cubed

375 g (12 oz) boned lamb shoulder, cubed

2 onions, thinly sliced

425 g (14 oz) canned tomatoes with their juice

1 bouquet garni

375 g (12 oz) garlic sausage or boiling ring, cut into 5 cm (2 inch) lengths

50 g (2 oz) fresh breadcrumbs

salt and pepper

2 tablespoons chopped parsley, to garnish

Serves 4

Preparation time: 30 minutes, plus soaking

Cooking time: 5 hours

1 Drain the soaked beans and put them into a large saucepan with the stock, pork rind, 4 whole garlic cloves, the carrot and the onion stuck with cloves. Cover, bring slowly to the boil and simmer for 1 hour. Strain off the liquid and reserve. Discard the carrot, onion and garlic. Put the beans and pork rind into a deep casserole.

2 Heat the oil in a large frying pan, add the pork, salt pork and lamb and brown on all sides. Lift out and add to the beans. Fry the sliced onions gently in the fat until softened. Stir in the tomatoes, the remaining garlic, crushed, the bean cooking liquid, the bouquet garni and salt and pepper to taste. Bring to the boil and pour over the beans.

3 Mix all the ingredients together, then cover the casserole and cook in a preheated oven, 170°C (325°F), Gas Mark 3, for 2½ hours. Remove the lid and carefully stir in the sausage. Taste and adjust the seasoning, if necessary. Sprinkle the crumbs evenly over the top and return to the oven, uncovered. Cook for a further 1 hour. The fat will rise to the surface to turn the crumbs into a crisp golden topping. Garnish with parsley.

■ Do not allow the cassoulet to get too dry during cooking; add a little more stock if necessary. The final dish should have a creamy consistency.

1 Have ready 6 ovenproof pots, approximately 400 ml (14 fl oz) size. Cut each fillet into 12 discs. Heat a little of the oil to smoking point in a frying pan. Quickly fry the lamb in small batches to seal and colour the meat. Place 4 pieces in each pot.

2 Brown the onions in the pan over a fairly fierce heat, adding a bit more oil, if necessary. Lift the onions out with a draining spoon and divide among the pots. Do the same with the celery, mushrooms and pearl barley.

3 Season each pot lightly with salt and pepper. Pour over enough wine and stock to cover. Arrange the potatoes neatly in overlapping circles on top of each pot and brush with melted butter. Cover the pots and cook in a preheated oven, 170°C (325°F), Gas Mark 3, for 1½ hours. Take off the lids, raise the temperature and cook for a further 20–30 minutes, or until the potatoes are golden-brown.

2 whole lamb fillets, trimmed and skinned

2 tablespoons olive or soy oil, for frying

24 button onions

3 inner stalks of celery, finely diced

18 button mushrooms

25 g (1 oz) pearl barley

150 ml (¼ pint) dry white wine

450 ml (¾ pint) chicken stock

6 potatoes, each weighing 125 g (4 oz), finely sliced

25 g (1 oz) butter, melted salt and pepper

Serves 6

Preparation time: 30 minutes

Cooking time: about 2½ hours

lancashire hot pots

steak & kidney pie

1 Put the steak, kidney, onion, celery and carrots in a large saucepan. Add the water, thyme and soy sauce with salt and pepper to taste. Bring to the boil, then lower the heat, cover and simmer for about 1½ hours, until the meat is tender.

2 Taste and add more seasoning if necessary. In a cup, blend the cornflour to a paste with a little water. Stir into the pan, cooking until the meat sauce is thickened and smooth. Stir in the parsley and leave to cool.

3 Roll out half the pastry on a lightly floured surface and line a 1.2 litre (2 pint) ovenproof dish or a 23 cm (9 inch) pie plate. Place the cooled meat mixture over the pastry. Position a pastry funnel in the middle of the pie. Dampen the edges of the pie with water. Roll out the remaining pastry, making a hole in the middle for the pastry funnel, and cover the pie. Trim the edges, then cut up the edges with a knife and flute to seal and decorate.

4 Reroll the pastry trimmings and cut into leaves. Attach to the pie with a little of the beaten egg. Brush the top of the pie with more egg and bake in a preheated oven, 220°C (425°F), Gas Mark 7, for 35–40 minutes, until the pastry is crisp and golden brown.

750 g (1½ lb) braising steak, cubed

250 g (8 oz) ox kidney, cored and trimmed

1 large onion, chopped

1 celery stick, chopped

2 carrots, chopped

300 ml (½ pint) water

½ teaspoon dried thyme

1 tablespoon soy sauce

1 tablespoon cornflour

2 tablespoons chopped parsley

375 g (12 oz) puff pastry, thawed if frozen

salt and pepper

beaten egg, to glaze

Serves 6

Preparation time: 25 minutes, plus cooling

Cooking time: about 2 hours 20 minutes

■ To make a fluted edge, place the forefinger of one hand in the inside edge of the pastry rim. Pinch the pastry around it with the thumb and forefinger of your other hand to make a pinched edge. Continue all round the edge of the pie.

lamb tagine

2 tablespoons oil

625 g (1¼ lb) lean lamb, diced

1 large onion, chopped

1 garlic clove, crushed

1 teaspoon ground ginger

1 teaspoon ground cinnamon

25 g (1 oz) plain flour

300 ml (½ pint) lamb stock

250 g (8 oz) pitted ready-to-eat prunes

salt and pepper

1 tablespoon toasted sesame seeds, to garnish

Serves 4
Preparation time: 15 minutes
Cooking time: 1 hour 40 minutes

1 Heat the oil in a frying pan, add the meat and cook until it is brown on all sides. Remove the meat from the pan with a slotted spoon and put into a casserole.

2 Fry the onion and garlic in the pan until soft, then add the spices and cook for 1 minute. Sprinkle the flour into the pan and cook for just 1 minute, then add the stock and season to taste. Bring to the boil, then pour over the lamb. Cover the casserole, and cook for 1 hour in a preheated oven, 180°C (350°F), Gas Mark 4. Add the prunes and cook for a further 30 minutes.

3 Transfer the lamb and prunes to a warmed serving dish and sprinkle with the sesame seeds before serving.

■ Traditionally, this Moroccan stew is cooked in a tagine, a round and shallow earthenware pot with a conical lid. These tagines can be bought in most kitchenware shops.

lamb dhansak

1 Heat the oil in a large frying pan and fry the onions, pepper, courgette and garlic until soft. Add the curry powder, paste and spices and fry for 1–2 minutes, then add the lamb. Fry over a moderate heat to seal and brown the lamb on all sides.

2 Add the tomatoes and lamb stock or water and bring to the boil. Transfer to an ovenproof casserole and put in a preheated oven, 190°C (375°F), Gas Mark 5, for 30 minutes.

3 Add the chopped coriander, sugar, garam marsala, drained lentils and salt to taste with a little water to moisten, if necessary. Return the casserole to the oven and cook for a further 40 minutes. Spoon off any excess oil before serving the dish, garnished with parsley sprigs.

4 tablespoons oil

2 onions, diced

1 yellow pepper, chopped

1 courgette, chopped

2 garlic cloves, chopped

2 tablespoons Madras curry powder

2 tablespoons mild curry paste

2 tablespoons ground coriander

1 teaspoon ground cumin

500 g (1 lb) lean lamb, diced

425 g (14 oz) canned chopped tomatoes and their juices

300 ml (½ pint) lamb stock or water

1 tablespoon chopped fresh coriander

1 tablespoon brown sugar

1 tablespoon garam masala

400 g (13 oz) canned red lentils, rinsed and drained

salt

parsley, to garnish

Serves 4

Preparation time: 20 minutes

Cooking time: 1½ hours

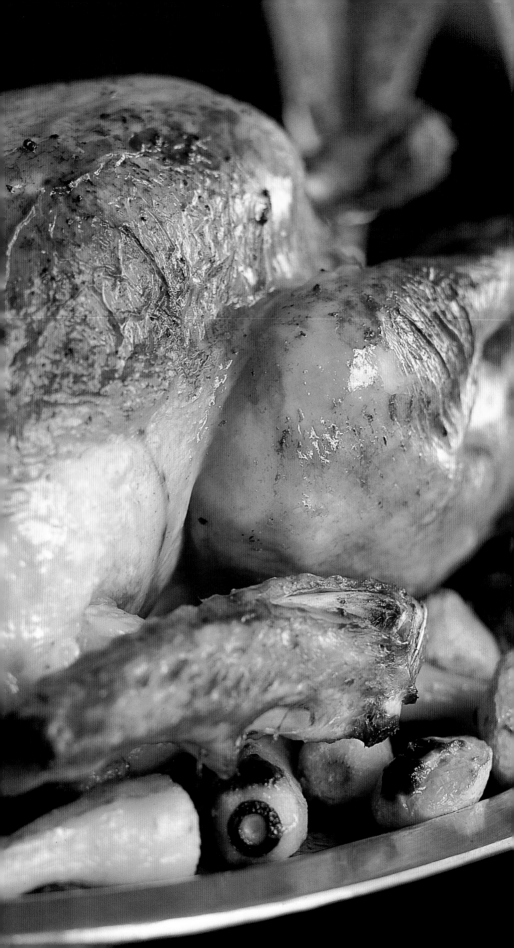

chicken
& poultry
dishes

125 g (4 oz) butter

3 large onions, finely sliced

10 peppercorns

10 cardamoms

5 cm (2 inch) piece cinnamon stick

5 cm (2 inch) piece of fresh root ginger, chopped

2 garlic cloves, finely chopped

1 teaspoon chilli powder

2 teaspoons paprika

1.5 kg (3 lb) chicken pieces, skinned

250 ml (8 fl oz) natural yogurt

salt

To Garnish:

lime wedges

parsley sprigs

1 Melt the butter in a deep, lidded frying pan or wok. Add the onions, peppercorns, cardamoms and cinnamon and fry until the onions are golden. Add the ginger, garlic, chilli powder, paprika and salt to taste and fry for 2 minutes, stirring occasionally.

2 Add the chicken pieces and fry until browned. Gradually add the yogurt, stirring constantly. Cover and cook for about 30 minutes. Serve hot, garnished with lime wedges and parsley sprigs.

Serves 6

Preparation time: 10 minutes

Cooking time: about 40 minutes

kashmiri chicken

chicken korma

1 Cook the onion and garlic gently in the butter or ghee in a large pan until soft. Add the saffron, coriander, chilli and half the water and cook for 3 minutes, stirring constantly.

2 Add the chicken and simmer for 20 minutes, covered. When the liquid has evaporated, continue to cook, stirring, until the chicken is golden brown.

3 Add the yogurt, cream, cumin, cloves, cardamons, poppy seeds and sesame seeds and season to taste. Add the remaining water, cover the pan and simmer gently until the chicken is tender – about 10 minutes. Add more water if the sauce becomes too dry. Transfer to a warmed serving dish and garnish with parsley and pistachios. Serve hot.

1 onion, finely sliced

2 garlic cloves, crushed

125 g (4 oz) butter or ghee

½ teaspoon saffron threads

3 teaspoons ground coriander

½ teaspoon ground chilli powder

300 ml (½ pint) water

750 g (1½ lb) skinless chicken breast, cut into chunks

50 ml (2 fl oz) plain yogurt

125 ml (4 fl oz) single cream

1 teaspoon white cumin seeds

10 cloves

4 brown cardamons

1 teaspoon poppy seeds

1 teaspoon sesame seeds

salt and pepper

To Garnish:

parsley sprigs

2 tablespoons roughly chopped pistachios

Serves 4
Preparation time: 15 minutes
Cooking time: 45 minutes

50

chicken kiev

1 Put the chicken breasts between 2 sheets of greaseproof paper and pound until thin using a rolling pin. Cut the garlic butter into 4 sticks. Put 1 stick in the centre of each chicken breast, then roll the chicken around the stick, folding in the sides so the butter is completely enclosed. If necessary, secure with wooden cocktail sticks.

2 Spread the seasoned flour out on one plate, the beaten eggs on a second plate and the breadcrumbs on a third. Coat the chicken breasts first in the seasoned flour, then in the beaten eggs, and then in the breadcrumbs. Press the breadcrumbs on firmly so that they stick. Repeat to give a second coating of egg and breadcrumbs (this helps to insulate the garlic butter so that the heat from the oil does not penetrate too early and melt the butter before the chicken is cooked). Chill for at least 1 hour.

3 Heat the oil in a deep-fat fryer to 180–190°C (350–375°F), or until a cube of bread browns in 30 seconds. Carefully lower the chicken parcels into the hot oil and deep-fry for 7–10 minutes until the breadcrumbs are golden brown and crisp on all sides, turning the chicken very carefully halfway through. Remove with a slotted spoon and drain on kitchen paper. Remove and discard the cocktail sticks. Serve hot with a mixed green salad.

4 large skinless chicken breast fillets

125 g (4 oz) garlic butter (see below)

20 g (¾ oz) seasoned plain flour

2 eggs, beaten

125 g (4 oz) dried white breadcrumbs

oil, for deep-frying

salt and pepper

mixed green salad, to serve

Serves 4
Preparation time: 30 minutes, plus freezing and chilling
Cooking time: 7–10 minutes

■ For garlic butter, beat 4 crushed garlic cloves and 2 tablespoons chopped fresh parsley into 125 g (4 oz) softened unsalted butter. Form into a wedge, wrap in non-stick baking parchment and freeze for at least 1 hour, until firm.

chicken marengo

1 Sprinkle the chicken with salt and pepper. Melt half of the butter in a pan, add the chicken and brown on all sides. Transfer to a casserole. Warm the brandy, pour over the chicken and ignite carefully. When the flames have died down, set the casserole aside.

2 Add the remaining butter to the pan and then add the onion and garlic. Fry gently until lightly coloured. Add the flour to the onions and cook for 1 minute. Add the tomatoes, wine and tomato purée and bring to the boil. Add the mushrooms, taste and adjust the seasoning, if necessary, and simmer for 2 minutes. Pour the sauce over the chicken and cover the casserole. Cook in a preheated oven, 180°C (350°F), Gas Mark 4, for about 45–50 minutes, or until tender.

3 To garnish, lightly fry the crayfish or prawns in butter. Arrange the chicken on plates, spoon the sauce over and garnish with the crayfish or prawns, egg and walnuts or olives.

2 kg (4 lb) chicken, cut into 8 skinless pieces

50 g (2 oz) butter

2 tablespoons brandy

1 onion, sliced

1–2 garlic cloves, crushed

2 tablespoons flour

425 g (14 oz) canned tomatoes, liquidized, puréed or very finely chopped

150 ml (¼ pint) dry white wine

1 tablespoon tomato purée

125 g (4 oz) button mushrooms, trimmed and halved

salt and pepper

To Garnish:

4 crayfish or 8 large whole prawns

25 g (1 oz) butter

2 hard-boiled eggs, shelled and quartered

few pickled walnut slices or black olives

Serves 4

Preparation time: 20 minutes

Cooking time: 1 hour 10 minutes

chicken véronique

1 Sprinkle the chicken pieces lightly with salt and pepper. Heat the butter and oil in a pan, add the chicken and fry until lightly browned all over. Transfer to a casserole.

2 Stir the flour into the pan juices, then add the wine and stock and bring to the boil. Add the lemon rind and juice, and pour over the chicken. Add the bay leaf. Cover the casserole and cook in a preheated oven, 180°C (350°F), Gas Mark 4, for 40 minutes.

3 Blend the cream with the egg yolk, add some of the sauce from the casserole, then stir back into the casserole with the grapes. Replace the lid and return to the oven for 15 minutes. Discard the bay leaf and serve the chicken garnished with small bunches of grapes.

4 skinless, part-boned chicken breasts

25 g (1 oz) butter

1 tablespoon oil

25 g (1 oz) plain flour

150 ml (¼ pint) medium white wine

150 ml (¼ pint) chicken stock

grated rind of ½ lemon

1 tablespoon lemon juice

1 bay leaf

150 ml (¼ pint) single cream

1 egg yolk

125 g (4 oz) green grapes, peeled, halved and deseeded, plus extra to garnish

salt and pepper

Serves 4
Preparation time: 15 minutes
Cooking time: 1 hour

1 Remove the giblets from the chicken and reserve for the gravy stock. Put 1 lemon and the bouquet garni inside the chicken cavity and truss the chicken securely. Place the chicken in an oiled roasting tin, pour over the olive oil and season. Place the tin in a preheated oven, 180°C (350°F), Gas Mark 4, and roast for 1½–1¾ hours or until the chicken is tender.

2 Prepare the bread sauce about 15 minutes before the chicken is cooked. Pour the milk into a pan and add the onion, cloves and bay leaves. Heat until the milk has almost reached boiling point. Stir in the breadcrumbs and butter. Remove from the heat and leave for 5 minutes. Add nutmeg and salt to taste.

3 Remove the chicken from the oven and place it on a serving dish. Pour off all but 2 tablespoons of fat from the pan, leaving the residue. Add the flour to the pan, and stir over a low heat until bubbling and golden. Gradually stir in the stock or wine. Season and simmer for 5 minutes. Serve hot with the sauce, gravy and lemon wedges.

1.5–2 kg (3–4 lb) oven-ready chicken with giblets

2 lemons

1 bouguet garni

4 tablespoons olive oil

salt and pepper

Bread Sauce:

600 ml (1 pint) milk

1 small onion, grated

pinch of ground cloves

pinch of ground bay leaves

75 g (3 oz) fresh white breadcrumbs

25 g (1 oz) butter

pinch of ground nutmeg

Gravy:

2 tablespoons plain flour

300 ml (½ pint) giblet stock or wine

Serves 6
Preparation time: 30 minutes
Cooking time: 1½–1¾ hours

roast chicken with bread sauce & gravy

1 Toss the chicken in the seasoned flour until coated. Melt the butter and oil in a frying pan, add the onions and fry for 5 minutes until softened and browned. Remove the onions from the pan and set aside. Add the chicken to the pan and fry for about 10 minutes until browned. Using a slotted spoon, transfer the chicken to a 1.5 litre (2½ pint) pie dish. Sprinkle the onions over the top.

2 Stir any remaining flour into the pan and cook for 1 minute. Gradually add the stock, stirring until the sauce is thick and smooth, scraping the base of the pan to incorporate any sediment. Stir in the lemon juice and bubble briefly. Stir in the double cream and parsley. Bring to the boil. Taste and adjust the seasoning, if necessary, then pour the sauce over the chicken.

3 Roll out the pastry to measure 5 cm (2 inches) larger than the pie dish. Cut off a 2.5 cm (1 inch) strip all round. Dampen the edge of the dish and attach the strip. Brush the strip with water and cover the pie with the remaining pastry. Pinch the edges of the pastry together and make a hole to allow the steam to escape. Brush the pastry with beaten egg or milk and sprinkle with sesame seeds. Bake in a preheated oven, 200°C (400°F), Gas Mark 6, for 30 minutes, then reduce the oven temperature to 180°C (350°F), Gas Mark 4, and bake for a further 45 minutes. Cover with foil if the pastry becomes too brown. Serve the pie hot.

chicken pie

8–10 boneless chicken thighs (about 625 g/1¼ lb total weight)

1 tablespoon seasoned plain flour

25 g (1 oz) butter

1 tablespoon olive oil

2 onions, chopped

300 g (½ pint) chicken stock

2 tablespoons lemon juice

150 ml (¼ pint) double cream

1 bunch of parsley, chopped

250 g (8 oz) shortcrust pastry, thawed if frozen

beaten egg or milk, to glaze

1 tablespoon sesame seeds

salt and pepper

Serves 4–6

Preparation time: 30 minutes

Cooking time: 1½ hours

crispy orange duck

1 Dry the duckling thoroughly inside and out with kitchen paper, then season the cavity. Tuck the tarragon and 4 of the kumquats inside the duckling, then place it on a rack over a roasting tin. With a needle, prick the duckling in several places to release the fat during cooking. Rub the skin with salt and roast in the centre of a preheated oven, 190°C (375°F), Gas Mark 5, for 1½ hours or until the skin is crisp and golden.

2 A few minutes before the duckling is cooked, cut the remaining kumquats in half and place them in a pan with the orange juice, sherry and honey. Bring to the boil and simmer gently for about 2 minutes, stirring constantly.

3 To serve, carve the duckling into 4 quarters, place on a warmed serving dish, spoon over the kumquats and serve with the green beans.

2 kg (4 lb) duckling

3 tarragon sprigs

250 g (8 oz) kumquats

1 tablespoon orange juice

3 tablespoons sherry

1 tablespoon clear honey

salt and pepper

green beans, to serve

Serves 4

Preparation time: 15 minutes

Cooking time: about 1½ hours

■ Kumquats are oval-shaped, small fruits with a distinctive citrus flavour. They do not need to be peeled; they can be eaten whole, skin and all.

1 First make the stuffing: heat the oil in a pan and fry the onion until soft. Stir in the walnuts, breadcrumbs, lemon rind, parsley and marjoram and season to taste. Bind with the egg.

2 Prick the duck all over with a fine skewer. Fill the body cavity with the stuffing. Truss the duck and set on a wire rack in a roasting tin. Mix the lemon juice and honey and brush the mixture over the duck. Season well and cook in a preheated oven, 220°C (425°F), Gas Mark 7, for 10 minutes, then reduce the heat to 190°C (375°F), Gas Mark 5, and cook for a further 2–2½ hours, depending on the size and allowing about 10–15 minutes resting time at the end.

3 Baste frequently during cooking, brushing with any remaining honey mixture. Remove from the oven and drain off all but 1 tablespoon of fat from the pan. Stir in the flour, blending with the cooking juices, add the stock and boil to thicken for the gravy. Garnish with watercress and serve with roasted root vegetables.

2.5–3 kg (5–6 lb) duckling

2 tablespoons lemon juice

2 tablespoons clear heather honey

2 tablespoons plain flour

300 ml (½ pint) duck or chicken stock

salt and pepper

watercress, to garnish

Walnut Stuffing:

1 tablespoon oil

1 onion, finely chopped

125 g (4 oz) walnuts, chopped

125 g (4 oz) fresh white breadcrumbs

grated rind of 1 lemon

1 tablespoon chopped parsley

1 teaspoon chopped marjoram

1 egg, beaten

Serves 4
Preparation time: 20 minutes
Cooking time: 2¼–2¾ hours

roast honey duck with walnut stuffing

coq au vin

1 Melt 25 g (1 oz) of the butter in a flameproof casserole, add the bacon and onions and cook gently until the onions begin to colour. Transfer to a plate.

2 Add the chicken joints to the casserole and brown on all sides. Warm the brandy, pour it over the chicken and set alight. When the flames have died down, return the bacon and onions to the casserole. Heat the wine in a saucepan and pour it over the chicken. Season to taste with salt and pepper. Stir in the garlic, bouquet garni and nutmeg. Cover the casserole and cook in a preheated oven, 180°C (350°F), Gas Mark 4, for 1 hour.

3 Stir the mushrooms into the casserole, re-cover and cook for a further 15 minutes. Remove the bouquet garni. Mix the flour and the remaining butter to a paste and whisk into the sauce in small pieces. Bring just to the boil, stirring. Stir in the yeast extract, if using; this deepens the colour. Adjust the seasoning and garnish with the croûtes and parsley.

50 g (2 oz) butter

125 g (4 oz) thick rindless streaky bacon, blanched and diced

12 pickling onions or shallots

1.5 kg (3 lb) roasting chicken, quartered

2 tablespoons brandy

1 bottle dry red wine

2 garlic cloves, crushed

1 bouquet garni

½ teaspoon ground nutmeg

250 g (8 oz) small button mushrooms

20 g (¾ oz) plain flour

1 teaspoon yeast extract (optional)

salt and pepper

To Garnish:

heart-shaped fried croûtes

chopped parsley

Serves 4

Preparation time: 40 minutes

Cooking time: 1½ hours

roast turkey

1 Remove the giblets from the turkey and use to make stock and the stuffing. Wash the inside of the turkey and dry thoroughly with kitchen paper. Pack the stuffing loosely into the neck of the bird. (Don't stuff the body cavity because this may prevent the bird from cooking through.) Place the onion in the body cavity, season to taste and place the bird in a large roasting tin and rub all over with butter. Add the oil to the tin and season the outside of the turkey with salt and pepper.

2 Once you have trussed the turkey place it in a large roasting tin and rub all over with butter. Add the oil to the tin and season the outside of the turkey with salt and pepper.

3 Roast in a preheated oven, 180°C (350°F), Gas Mark 4, for 3–3¼ hours, basting from time to time. Cover with greaseproof paper or foil when sufficiently browned. Check if it is ready by inserting a skewer into the thickest part of the thigh; the juices should run clear. If they are pink, cook for a further 15 minutes and test again. Repeat as necessary.

4 Transfer the turkey to a large dish. Pour off the fat from the juices and use if making gravy. Arrange the turkey on a warmed serving platter and serve with gravy, bread sauce and an assortment of seasonal vegetables.

5–6 kg (10–12 lb) oven-ready turkey, with giblets

Pecan Stuffing (see page 61)

1 small onion, peeled and halved

40 g (1½ oz) butter or margarine, softened

2 tablespoons vegetable oil

salt and pepper

Serves 8

Preparation time: 20 minutes

Cooking time: 3–3¼ hours

■ Traditional accompaniments to roast turkey are bread sauce (see page 54), roast potatoes and roasted parsnips. The vegetables can be roasted in the turkey juices around the bird, if liked. Remember to allow 10–15 minutes resting time before carving to let the meat relax. Carving straight from the oven can result in tough meat.

pecan stuffing

1 Put the heart and liver into a saucepan and cover with water. Bring to the boil and simmer for 10 minutes. Chop both finely and set aside to cool.

2 Place the meat in a bowl and stir in the breadcrumbs, nuts, egg, spices, parsley and celery salt.

3 Melt the butter in a saucepan, add the mushrooms and onion and cook over a moderate heat, stirring frequently, for about 5 minutes until softened. Stir into the meat mixture, add the sherry and season to taste.

heart and liver from the turkey

50 g (2 oz) fresh breadcrumbs

50 g (2 oz) shelled pecan nuts, finely chopped

1 egg, hardboiled and chopped

pinch each of grated nutmeg, ground mace and thyme

1 tablespoon chopped parsley

pinch of celery salt

40 g (1½ oz) butter

50 g (2 oz) mushrooms, finely chopped

1 small onion, chopped

2 tablespoons dry sherry

salt and pepper

Preparation time: 5 minutes

Cooking time: 15–20 minutes

salmon steaks with orange sauce ●

sole véronique ●

lemon sole with citrus and wild rice ●

tuna fish cakes ●

salad niçoise with hot grilled tuna ●

cheesy fish pie ●

skate with black butter ●

grilled plaice with a herb crust ●

shellfish paella ●

lobster thermidor ●

moules marinière ●

fish & shellfish

salmon steaks
with orange sauce

1 Sprinkle the orange juice over the salmon steaks, season with pepper and set aside at room temperature for at least 15 minutes.

2 Brush a grill rack with oil. Brush the salmon steaks with half the melted butter and cook for 4 minutes under a preheated grill. Turn the steaks over, brush them with the remaining butter and grill for a further 5 minutes.

3 To make the sauce, put all the ingredients except the oil in a blender. Blend for 2–3 seconds. With the machine still running, pour in the oil slowly. Taste the sauce and adjust the seasoning if necessary. Serve the salmon and orange sauce with orange wedges and a steamed green vegetable, such as asparagus.

2 tablespoons orange juice

4 salmon steaks, about 125 g (4 oz) each

vegetable oil, for brushing

50 g (½ oz) butter, melted

orange wedges, to serve

salt and pepper

Orange Sauce:

1 egg

pinch of mustard powder

2 teaspoons grated orange rind

1 tablespoon orange juice

125 ml (4 fl oz) vegetable oil

Serves 4
Preparation time: 10 minutes, plus marinating
Cooking time: 10 minutes

sole véronique

1 Place the sole fillets in a lightly greased ovenproof dish. Surround them with the onion slices, bay leaf, parsley, fish stock and season to taste.

2 Pour in the wine just to cover, and bake in a preheated oven, 160°C (325°F), Gas Mark 3, for up to 20 minutes, according to the thickness of the fillets. Transfer the fillets to a warmed serving dish and keep warm. Strain the cooking liquid into a pan and reduce it to 6 tablespoons.

3 For the sauce, melt the butter in a saucepan, add the flour and stir for 2 minutes over a low heat. Remove from the heat and gradually stir in the milk and reduced stock and season with salt and pepper. Return the pan to a low heat, bring to the boil and cook for 2–3 minutes, stirring constantly until the sauce thickens. Remove from the heat and stir in the double cream. Coat the fillets with this sauce, and garnish with the grapes and sprigs of dill. Remove the bay leaf before serving. Serve at once with a selection of vegetables.

8 sole fillets, skinned and rolled

1 onion, sliced

1 bay leaf

few parsley sprigs

150 ml (¼ pint) fish stock

150–300 ml (¼–½ pint) dry white wine

salt and pepper

Sauce:

25 g (1 oz) butter

25 g (1 oz) plain flour

150 ml (¼ pint) milk

150 ml (¼ pint) double cream

To Garnish:

about 20 seedless black or white grapes, halved

dill sprigs

Serves 4
Preparation time: 15 minutes
Cooking time: about 40 minutes

1 Cook the wild rice in a large pan of boiling salted water for about 40–45 minutes, or according to packet instructions, until tender.

2 Meanwhile, melt the butter in a large saucepan over a moderate heat, add the shallots and cook for 3 minutes until soft. Add the wine, orange juice, orange rind and redcurrant jelly, if using. Bring to the boil, then boil until reduced by half. Season with salt and pepper and add honey to taste. Cover the saucepan and keep warm.

3 Coat the sole fillets with the flour and season to taste. Heat the oil in a frying pan, add the sole fillets, in batches, and cook for 3 minutes on each side or until cooked through. Remove from the pan and keep warm.

4 Drain the rice and stir in the orange segments. Spoon on to warmed serving plates and place the fish on top. Pour the sauce over the fish, garnish with parsley and serve.

250 g (8 oz) wild rice

25 g (1 oz) butter

4 shallots, finely chopped

300 ml (10 fl oz) dry white wine

250 ml (8 fl oz) orange juice

2 teaspoons grated orange rind

3 teaspoons redcurrant jelly (optional)

clear honey, to taste

8 lemon sole fillets

2 tablespoons flour

sunflower oil, for shallow-frying

2 oranges peeled, and cut into segments

salt and pepper

parsley, to garnish

Serves 4

Preparation time: 10–15 minutes

Cooking time: 45 minutes

lemon sole with citrus and wild rice

tuna fish cakes

1 Mash the potatoes with the butter or margarine, then mix in the tuna, parsley, half the beaten egg and salt and pepper to taste.

2 Chill the mixture for 20 minutes, then place on a floured surface and shape into a roll. Cut into 8 slices and shape each into a flat round, about 6 cm (2½ inches) in diameter. Dip into the remaining egg, then coat with breadcrumbs.

3 Heat the oil in a frying pan, add the fish cakes in batches and fry for 2–3 minutes on each side or until golden brown and heated through. Garnish each fish cake with a parsley sprig. Serve with lemon wedges.

300 g (10 oz) potatoes, boiled

25 g (1 oz) butter or margarine

300 g (10 oz) canned tuna, drained and flaked

2 tablespoons chopped parsley

2 eggs, beaten

75 g (3 oz) dry breadcrumbs

oil, for shallow-frying

salt and pepper

parsley sprigs, to garnish

lemon wedges, to serve

Serves 4

Preparation time: 15 minutes, plus chilling

Cooking time: about 20 minutes

■ These fish cakes are even more tasty when accompanied by a simple tomato sauce. Place a 425 g (14 oz) can of chopped tomatoes, 1 crushed garlic clove, 3 tablespoons olive oil and 1 teaspoon of sugar in a saucepan. Bring to the boil and simmer gently for 15 minutes. Season to taste with salt, pepper and lemon juice.

4 x 2.5 cm (1 inch) thick tuna steaks

Marinade:

2 tablespoons olive oil

1 tablespoon red wine vinegar

1 shallot, finely chopped

1 garlic clove, crushed

freshly ground black pepper

salad niçoise with hot grilled tuna

Salad:

3 hardboiled eggs, quartered

6–8 lettuce leaves

2 tomatoes, sliced

10–12 slices peeled cucumber, deseeded

4 green pepper rings

8 chicory leaves

8 watercress sprigs

1 small onion, sliced

8 black or green olives

8 anchovy fillets

1 tablespoon capers

1 Cut each piece of fish across the middle into 2 pieces. Mix the marinade ingredients together, then pour over the fish, cover and leave to marinate overnight.

2 Assemble the salad on 4 plates. Put all the dressing ingredients into a screw-top jar and shake until well mixed. Taste and adjust the seasoning. Drizzle some of the dressing over each salad.

3 Remove the fish from the marinade and sear under a hot grill or in a lightly-oiled frying pan. Baste with the marinade and cook for 2 minutes only on each side. Arrange the hot pieces of tuna on top of the salad and serve immediately.

■ If fresh tuna is not available, use halibut or turbot pieces for this salad.

Dressing:

3 tablespoons olive or soy oil

1½ tablespoons red wine vinegar

1 teaspoon French mustard

1 small garlic clove, finely chopped

Serves 4
Preparation time: 40 minutes, plus marinating
Cooking time: 4 minutes

cheesy fish pie

1 Put the fish into a shallow pan with the bay leaf, peppercorns and half of the milk. Bring to the boil and simmer, covered, for 15 minutes or until the fish flakes easily. In another pan, heat the oil and fry the onions for 15 minutes until soft and lightly golden. Spoon into an ovenproof dish and arrange the fish on top. Strain the milk from the fish pan and reserve.

2 Put the potatoes in a saucepan, sprinkling each layer with a few slivers of garlic, some nutmeg and salt and pepper. Cover with the remaining milk, bring to the boil, then simmer gently for about 8–10 minutes until they are just done.

3 Put 4 of the eggs into a small pan, cover with water and boil for about 10 minutes until hard. Add the tomatoes to the oil left in the onion pan and stir-fry over a high heat for 2–3 minutes. Arrange the tomatoes on top of the fish and sprinkle with the dill.

4 Drain the potatoes, reserving the milk. Cool the eggs, then shell and slice. Arrange the slices over the tomatoes, then cover with the potatoes. Beat the remaining 2 eggs well, then whisk in the 2 lots of milk. Pour over the dish, adding extra milk if necessary, so the liquid is level with the potatoes. Sprinkle over the cheese. Cook in a preheated oven, 180°C (350°F), Gas Mark 4 , for 20 minutes. Garnish with dill sprigs and serve.

500 g (1 lb) skinless white fish fillets, (e.g. cod or haddock)

1 bay leaf

6 white peppercorns

1.2 litres (2 pints) milk

2 tablespoons olive oil

2 large onions, finely sliced

500 g (1 lb) potatoes, finely sliced

1 garlic clove, sliced

pinch of ground nutmeg

6 large eggs

500 g (1 lb) tomatoes, skinned and finely sliced

½ teaspoon dried dill

50 g (2 oz) Cheddar cheese, grated

salt and pepper

dill sprigs, to garnish

Serves 6

Preparation time: 20–25 minutes

Cooking time: about 40 minutes

skate with black butter

1 Place the water, 2 tablespoons of the vinegar, the lemon rind, onion, peppercorns, carrot and salt in a saucepan. Bring to the boil and simmer for 30 minutes, then take off the heat and allow to cool (plunging the pan into a basin of very cold water will speed up this process).

2 Put the fish in one layer in a large pan. Strain the cooled bouillon over, and slowly bring to the boil. Allow to bubble for 5 seconds, then cook over the lowest possible heat – the liquid should barely simmer – for 12–15 minutes, until the fish is cooked. Transfer the fish to a hot serving dish.

3 Melt the butter in a frying pan and cook over a medium heat until a deep golden colour (despite the name, the butter should not turn black, as it would be burnt). Cook for a few seconds only, then pour it over the fish. Quickly pour the remaining vinegar into the pan and bring to the boil over a high heat. Stir in the capers and chopped parsley and pour over the fish immediately. Garnish with parsley sprigs and serve hot.

1.2 litres (2 pints) cold water

4 tablespoons wine vinegar

5 cm (2 inch) piece of lemon rind

1 onion, sliced

12 white peppercorns, lightly crushed

1 carrot, sliced

¼ teaspoon finely ground sea salt

6 skate wings, about 250 g (8 oz) each, rinsed in cold water

125 g (4 oz) unsalted butter

1 tablespoon capers, chopped

3 tablespoons finely chopped parsley

parsley sprigs, to garnish

Serves 6

Preparation time: 10 minutes, plus cooling

Cooking time: 45 minutes

grilled plaice with a herb crust

1 Roughly tear the bread into pieces, place in a food processor and make into breadcrumbs. Put the breadcrumbs into a bowl with the herbs and mix together. Season with salt and add a squeeze of lemon juice. Stir in enough of the oil and melted butter to make the mixture moist.

2 Meanwhile, put the plaice fillets, skin side down, on a sheet of greased foil on a grill rack. Season to taste, dot with butter and spread with the herb mixture. Place the fillets under a pre-heated moderate grill and cook for about 10 minutes until the fish are cooked through.

3 Arrange the plaice fillets on top of the tomato slices or on a bed of onions and tomatoes or other vegetables and serve at once.

75 g (3 oz) sun-dried tomato bread

3 tablespoons finely chopped mixed parsley, tarragon and chives

squeeze of lemon juice

3 tablespoons olive oil, plus extra for greasing

25 g (1 oz) butter, melted

4 plaice fillets

2 onions, thinly sliced

4 yellow tomatoes, thinly sliced

salt and pepper

Serves 2

Preparation time: 15 minutes

Cooking time: 10 minutes

shellfish paella

1 Clean the mussels, scrubbing them well and removing the beards. Discard any that are open. Cook in a little water in a large pan until they have opened. Discard any that have not opened. Reserve the cooking liquid. Shell the lobster or skin and bone the monkfish and cut up the flesh. Slice the squid into thin rings and slice the scallops. Slice the red and green peppers into thin strips and gently cook in 2 tablespoons of the olive oil. Remove from the pan and keep warm.

2 Add the sliced squid and scallops (and monkfish if used) to the pan and turn them gently as they cook, then remove and keep warm. In a large paella dish or shallow pan, gently cook the onion in the remaining olive oil until transparent. Add the rice and fry gently for a few more minutes, then pour in the wine, fish stock and reserved mussel liquid. Bring to a simmering point, add the saffron powder and give a few careful stirs; then add the bay leaves.

3 After about 10–15 minutes the rice, now a saffron yellow, should have absorbed the stock and you can stir in the petit pois. Then add the prawns, all the reserved fish and shellfish and the red and green pepper, and, again, give a few gentle stirs. Let the paella heat through, tasting and adjusting the seasoning, if necessary. Remove the bay leaves before serving.

1.8 litres (3 pints) mussels

1 medium cooked lobster or 250 g (8 oz) monkfish

375 g (12 oz) prepared squid

12 prepared scallops

1 red pepper, cored and deseeded

1 green pepper, cored and deseeded

6 tablespoons olive oil

2 large Spanish onions, finely chopped

1 kg (2 lb) long-grain rice

150 ml (¼ pint) dry white wine

1 litre (1¾ pints) fish stock

2–3 teaspoons saffron powder

2 bay leaves

250 g (8 oz) frozen petit pois

500 g (1 lb) peeled cooked prawns

salt and pepper

Serves 8

Preparation time: 35 minutes

Cooking time: about 25 minutes

lobster thermidor

1 Lay the lobsters on their backs and, with a strong sharp knife, cut in half lengthways, taking care not to damage the shells. Alternatively, ask your fishmonger to do this for you. Extract the meat from the body and claws. Reserve the lobster shells and oil them lightly. Chop up the lobster flesh, and gently sauté it in 25 g (1 oz) of the butter for 4 minutes, turning all the time, then remove from the pan and keep warm.

2 Melt the remaining butter in a saucepan and gently cook the shallot, then add the flour and cook for 1–2 minutes. Remove from the heat and gradually stir in the wine and the stock. Return to a low heat and bring to the boil, stirring constantly until thickened. Cook for 2–3 minutes. Add the mustard, salt and pepper to taste, and a little lemon juice, if liked.

3 Fold the lobster flesh into this sauce, and pour the mixture into the lobster shells. Sprinkle the browned breadcrumbs over the mixture in the shells, and brown under a hot grill until golden and bubbling. Sprinkle with the parsley and garnish with the lime twists and lemon geranium sprigs, if using.

2 cooked lobsters, each weighing about 750 g (1½ lb)

75 g (3 oz) butter

1 shallot, finely chopped

50 g (2 oz) plain flour

4 tablespoons dry white wine

300 ml (½ pint) fish stock

1 teaspoon prepared English mustard

2 tablespoons lemon juice (optional)

4 tablespoons wholemeal breadcrumbs, browned in a little butter

salt and pepper

To Garnish:

1 tablespoon chopped parsley

lime twists

lemon geranium sprigs (optional)

Serves 4
Preparation time: 20 minutes
Cooking time: 15 minutes

1 Scrub and clean all the mussels, removing any beards. Place the mussels, discarding any that are open, in a saucepan with the shallots, onion, parsley, wine and butter. Bring to the boil, cover and simmer for about 5 minutes, shaking the pan occasionally, until the shells are open. Remove the mussels with a slotted spoon and discard any mussels that do not open. Pile the mussels into a warmed serving bowl and keep hot.

2 Strain the cooking liquid into another pan. Bring to the boil and continue boiling for 1 minute. Season to taste, then pour over the mussels.

3 Garnish with parsley and serve with warm French bread.

2.4 litres (4 pints) fresh mussels

2 shallots

1 onion, chopped

50 g (2 oz) chopped parsley

300 ml (½ pint) dry white wine

50 g (2 oz) butter

salt and pepper

chopped parsley, to garnish

Serves 4

Preparation time: 20 minutes

Cooking time: 6 minutes

moules marinière

■ To make the sauce richer, stir in 3 tablespoons of single cream just before serving. Do not allow the sauce to boil after the cream has been added.

desserts & baking

mocha pots

1 Break the chocolate into a heatproof bowl. Add the butter and coffee powder and place the bowl over a saucepan of hot water. Heat gently until melted, being careful not to let the water in the pan boil. Beat in the egg yolks until smooth. Off the heat, stir in the liqueur.

2 Whisk the egg whites until stiff and fold into the chocolate mixture. Spoon into 4 coffee cups or small glasses. Chill until set.

3 Just before serving, decorate each mocha pot with a rosette of whipped cream and crystallized violets, if using. Serve at once.

75 g (3 oz) plain chocolate

25 g (1 oz) butter

1 tablespoon instant coffee powder

3 eggs, separated

1 tablespoon chocolate or coffee liqueur

To Decorate:

whipped cream

crystallized violet petals (optional)

Serves 4
Preparation time: 15 minutes, plus chilling
Cooking time: 3 minutes

old english trifle

1 Cut the sponge cakes in half, spread with jam and sandwich together. Cut each into 6–8 pieces and place in the bottom of a serving bowl. Pour the sherry and brandy over.

2 Heat the milk until it steams. Beat the eggs and sugar together and pour on the hot milk. Mix, return to the pan and heat gently, stirring, until the custard thickens. Allow the mixture to cool slightly, then pour it over the sponge cakes and leave until cold.

3 Spread two-thirds of the cream over the top of the trifle.

4 Decorate the trifle with rosettes made from the remaining cream and angelica leaves. Chill the trifle until required. Decorate it with edible flowers just before serving, if liked.

8 trifle sponge cakes

2–3 tablespoons seedless raspberry jam

4–5 tablespoons sherry

4–5 tablespoons brandy

600 ml (1 pint) milk

4 eggs

25 g (1 oz) caster sugar

450 ml (¾ pint) whipping cream, whipped to form soft peaks

To Serve:

small piece of angelica, cut into leaves

edible flowers (optional)

Serves 8–10

Preparation time: 20–25 minutes, plus cooling

Cooking time: 5–8 minutes

shortbread

1 Cream the butter and sugar together until light and fluffy. Sieve in the cornflour and plain flour and mix well to combine. Press into an oblong tin approximately 30 x 20 cm (12 x 8 inches) and mark with the prongs of a fork.

2 Bake in a preheated oven, 140°C (275°F), Gas Mark 1, for 30 minutes, then reduce the oven temperature to 120°C (250°F), Gas Mark ½ and cook for a further 1–1½ hours.

3 Remove the shortbread from the oven and cut into 32 even-sized fingers. Sprinkle with caster sugar and leave to cool slightly in the tin before transferring to a wire rack to cool until firm. Store in an airtight tin.

250 g (8 oz) butter

125 g (4 oz) caster sugar, plus extra for sprinkling

50 g (2 oz) cornflour

300 g (10 oz) plain flour

Makes 32 fingers
Preparation time: 15 minutes
Cooking time: 1½–2 hours

■ This mixture can also be rolled out thinly and cut into circular biscuits. Sometimes a little semolina is added to give a more crunchy texture.

baked scones

1 Sift the flour, cream of tartar, soda and salt into a mixing bowl and rub in the fat with your fingertips until the mixture resembles fine breadcrumbs. Stir in the sugar and add enough milk to mix to a soft dough.

2 Turn the dough on to a floured surface, knead lightly and roll out to 2 cm (¾ inch) thick. Cut into 5 cm (2 inch) rounds.

3 Place the rounds on a floured baking sheet and brush with milk. Bake in a preheated oven, 220°C (425°F), Gas Mark 7, for 10 minutes. Transfer to a wire rack to cool. Serve with butter or whipped cream and jam.

250 g (8 oz) plain flour

1 teaspoon cream of tartar

½ teaspoon bicarbonate of soda

pinch of salt

50 g (2 oz) butter or margarine

25 g (1 oz) caster sugar

125 ml (4 fl oz) milk, plus extra for glazing

To Serve:

butter or whipped cream

jam

Makes about 10

Preparation time: 10 minutes

Cooking time: 10 minutes

---

pecan pie

1 To make the pastry, sift the flour into a bowl, add the butter and rub it in with your fingertips until the mixture resembles fine breadcrumbs. Stir in the sugar then add enough water to make a firm dough. Knead the pastry dough briefly on a lightly floured surface, then roll out and line a 28 x 18 cm (11 x 7 inch) shallow Swiss roll tin. Chill the pastry-lined tin for 30 minutes.

2 To make the filling, mix the sugar, dark treacle or molasses, syrup, butter and vanilla essence in a bowl. Stir in the lemon rind and beaten eggs and mix well. Chop half the pecans and add to the filling mixture. Pour into the prepared pie crust.

3 Arrange the remaining pecans over the top of the pie. Bake in a preheated oven, 180°C (350°F), Gas Mark 4, for 45–50 minutes, until the pie shell is golden brown and the filling has set. Leave to cool, then cut into squares to serve.

Shortcrust Pastry:

300 g (10 oz) plain flour

250 g (8 oz) chilled butter, diced

4 tablespoons sugar

4–6 tablespoons cold water

Filling:

100 g (3½ oz) demerara sugar

4 tablespoons dark treacle or molasses

4 tablespoons golden syrup

6 tablespoons butter, melted

1 teaspoon vanilla essence

grated rind of 1 lemon

4 eggs, beaten

175 g (6 oz) pecan nuts

Serves 8–10

Preparation time: 25 minutes, plus chilling

Cooking time: 45–50 minutes

■ To make a chocolate and pecan pie, add 2 tablespoons of sifted unsweetened cocoa powder to the filling mixture. Sprinkle 50 g (2 oz) of grated chocolate over the cooked baked pie.

1 To make the pastry, sift the flour and salt into a bowl. Rub in the fat with your fingertips until the mixture resembles breadcrumbs. Add the water, slowly, to make a stiff dough. Knead the dough lightly then put it in a polythene bag and chill for 20–30 minutes.

2 Layer the apples with the sugar and spices in a 900 ml (1½ pint) pie dish. Roll out the dough on a lightly floured surface to a circle 5 cm (2 inches) larger than the dish. Cut off a strip all round and use to cover the damped rim of the dish; brush with water. Cut the dough into strips and make a lattice covering over the apples, sealing the edges. Trim the edges. Brush with water, sprinkle with the sugar to glaze, and bake in a preheated oven, 200°C (400°F), Gas Mark 6, for 30–40 minutes.

3 To make the crème à la vanille, cream the egg yolks with the cornflour and sugar. Bring the milk to the boil, pour on to the egg mixture and stir. Heat gently, stirring until the mixture coats the back of a spoon. Add the vanilla, then strain. Serve with the pie.

Pastry:

300 g (10 oz) plain flour

pinch of salt

125 g (4 oz) butter or margarine, diced

3 tablespoons water

Filling:

750 g (1½ lb) tart green apples, peeled, cored and thinly sliced

100 g (3½ oz) soft brown sugar

1 teaspoon allspice

4 cloves

water and sugar, to glaze

Crème à la Vanille:

2 egg yolks

1 teaspoon cornflour

2 tablespoons sugar

300 ml (½ pint) milk

½ teaspoon vanilla essence

Serves 4–6

Preparation time: 20 minutes, plus chilling

Cooking time: 30–40 minutes

spiced apple pie

banoffi pie

1 For the pie base, melt the butter in a pan and stir in the crushed digestive biscuits. Press the mixture evenly over the base and sides of a 20 cm (8 inch) round, deep flan tin. Chill until firm.

2 For the filling, put the butter and sugar in a pan. Heat gently, stirring, until the butter has melted. Stir in the evaporated milk and bring to the boil. Lower the heat and simmer for about 15 minutes, stirring occasionally, until the mixture becomes a caramel colour. Pour into the crumb base, cool, then chill until set.

3 Slice the bananas and toss them in the lemon juice. Reserve a quarter of the bananas for the decoration and spread the rest over the filling. Beat the cream and spread gently over the top. Decorate with the reserved bananas and sprinkle with the grated chocolate.

Biscuit Base:

125 g (4 oz) butter

250 g (8 oz) digestive biscuits, crushed

Filling:

175 g (6 oz) butter

150 g (5 oz) sugar

475 ml (16 fl oz) evaporated milk

2 bananas

1 tablespoon lemon juice

150 ml (¼ pint) double cream

25 g (1 oz) plain chocolate, grated

Serves 6–8

Preparation time: 30 minutes, plus chilling

Cooking time: 25 minutes

lemon meringue pie

1 Put the flour in a bowl, add the butter and rub in with your fingertips until the mixture resembles fine breadcrumbs. Stir in the sugar and ground hazelnuts, then add the egg yolk and enough cold water to mix to a firm dough. Knead the pastry dough briefly on a lightly floured surface, then roll out and use to line a 20 cm (8 inch) flan tin. Chill for 30 minutes, then fill with crumpled foil and bake in a preheated oven, 200°C (400°F), Gas Mark 6, for 15 minutes. Remove the foil and bake the tart shell for a further 5 minutes.

2 For the filling, mix the cornflour and sugar in a saucepan. Add the water, lemon rind and juice, and stir until well blended. Bring to the boil, stirring until thickened and smooth. Cool slightly. Beat the egg yolks in a bowl, then beat in 2 tablespoons of the lemon sauce. Return this mixture to the pan and cook gently until the sauce has thickened further. Let the sauce cool slightly, then pour it into the pastry case.

3 For the meringue, beat the egg whites in a clean bowl until stiff and dry. Beat in 1 tablespoon of the sugar, then fold in the rest. Spread the meringue mixture over the tart to cover the filling. Return to the oven for 10 minutes, until the meringue is golden. Serve the tart warm or cold.

250 g (8 oz) plain flour

150 g (5 oz) chilled butter, diced

50 g (2 oz) caster sugar

65 g (2½ oz) ground hazelnuts

1 egg yolk, beaten

2–3 tablespoons water

Filling:

6 tablespoons cornflour

100 g (3½ oz) sugar

350 ml (12 fl oz) water

grated rind and juice of 2 lemons

3 egg yolks

Meringue:

3 egg whites

150 g (5 oz) sugar

Serves 6

Preparation time: 35 minutes, plus chilling

Cooking time: 35 minutes

christmas pudding

1 Sift the flour and spices into a large mixing bowl. Add the dry ingredients, carrot and apple. Stir well. Stir in the eggs, grated orange rind and juice and Guinness. Mix together well. Cover and leave overnight in a cool, dry place.

2 Spoon into a lightly greased 1.8 litre (3 pint) pudding basin. Cover with buttered foil with a centre pleat and steam in a saucepan of boiling water for 4 hours, checking the water level from time to time. Set the pudding aside in the basin until it is completely cold. Remove it from the basin, wrap it in greaseproof paper and then foil and store in a cool, dry place for up to 3 months.

3 To serve the pudding, unwrap it and re-steam it in the basin for 1 hour. Turn out of the pudding basin and serve it. To flame the pudding, warm the brandy or rum in a small saucepan. Pour the alcohol over the pudding and ignite immediately.

■ This mixture will also make two small puddings. Use two 900 ml (1½ pint) pudding basins and steam the puddings for 2 hours. To re-heat them, steam for 30–45 minutes.

175 g (6 oz) plain flour

1 teaspoon mixed spice

1 teaspoon ground nutmeg

1 teaspoon ground cinnamon

50 g (2 oz) fresh white breadcrumbs

125 g (4 oz) suet

125 g (4 oz) brown sugar

125 g (4 oz) sultanas

125 g (4 oz) currants

125 g (4 oz) raisins

125 g (4 oz) cut mixed peel

125 g (4 oz) almonds, chopped

125 g (4 oz) carrot, grated

125 g (4 oz) apple, grated

2 eggs, beaten

grated rind and juice of 1 small orange

150 ml (¼ pint) Guinness

3 tablespoons brandy or rum, to flame (optional)

Serves 10–12

Preparation time: 20 minutes, plus standing

Cooking time: 4 hours, then 1 hour before serving

bread & butter pudding

1 Use 15 g (½ oz) of the butter to grease a 1.2 litre (2 pint) ovenproof serving dish.

2 Butter the bread and spread with apricot jam. Cut into small triangles. Layer the bread in the dish, sprinkling mixed peel and sultanas between the layers. Heat the milk and sugar to just below boiling point. Whisk in the beaten eggs, then strain over the bread and butter. Leave to soak for 30 minutes.

3 Place the dish in a bain marie (see below). Bake in a preheated oven, 180°C (350°F), Gas Mark 4, for 45 minutes, then increase the heat to 190°C (375°F), Gas Mark 5, and cook for a further 10–15 minutes until crisp and golden on top and just set. Serve at once with cream, if liked.

40 g (1½ oz) butter

4 slices white bread, crusts removed

4 tablespoons apricot jam

25 g (1 oz) cut mixed peel

25 g (1 oz) sultanas

450 ml (¾ pint) milk

2 tablespoons sugar

2 eggs, beaten

Serves 4

Preparation time: 10 minutes, plus soaking

Cooking time: about 1 hour

■ To make a bain marie, place the dish in a large roasting tin and pour boiling water into the tin to come at least halfway up the sides of the dish.

apricot & almond crumble

1 If using fresh apricots, cut in half and remove the stones and, if you wish, crack a few of the stones and remove the kernels. Place the fresh apricots and kernels or the cooked dried apricots in the bottom of a 1.2 litre (2 pint) buttered pie dish. Sprinkle the granulated sugar and almonds over, if using.

2 Mix the flour, caster sugar and ground almonds together and rub in the butter until the mixture resembles soft breadcrumbs. Spread lightly over the fruit.

3 Bake in a preheated oven, 200°C (400°F), Gas Mark 6, for 20 minutes, then reduce the oven temperature to 180°C (350°F), Gas Mark 4, and cook for a further 20–30 minutes until golden brown. Serve the crumble hot with custard or lightly whipped cream, if liked.

500–750 g (1–1½ lb) fresh apricots or 375 g (12 oz) dried apricots, soaked overnight and cooked until tender

25 g (1 oz) granulated sugar (optional)

50 g (2 oz) blanched almonds (optional)

125 g (4 oz) plain flour

75 g (3 oz) caster sugar

125 g (4 oz) ground almonds

175 g (6 oz) unsalted butter

Serves 4–6

Preparation time: 15–25 minutes, plus soaking (if using dried apricots)

Cooking time: 40–50 minutes

bakewell tart

1 Roll out the pastry on a lightly floured clean surface and use to line a 20 cm (8 inch) flan ring or dish. Prick the base lightly and spread the jam over.

2 Beat the eggs and sugar together until they are thick and creamy. Beat in the butter a little at a time, then fold in the ground almonds. Combine well, then pour the mixture into the prepared pastry case.

3 Place on a hot baking sheet and bake in a preheated oven, 200°C (400°F), Gas Mark 6, for 25–30 minutes until set and golden brown. Serve the tart hot or cold.

½ quantity Shortcrust Pastry (see Pecan Pie, page 84)

2 tablespoons raspberry jam

4 eggs

125 g (4 oz) caster sugar

125 g (4 oz) unsalted butter, melted and cooled

125 g (4 oz) ground almonds

Serves 5–6
Preparation time: 30 minutes
Cooking time: 25–30 minutes

sussex pond pudding

1 Sift the flour into a bowl. Stir in the suet and add the water to make a soft dough. Roll out two-thirds of the dough to line a greased 1.5 litre (2½ pint) pudding basin.

2 Put half the sugar and dried fruit into the lined basin. Prick the lemon all over with a skewer and place upright on top. Cover with the butter in one piece and sprinkle over the remaining sugar and fruit.

3 Roll out the rest of the pastry to make a lid. Moisten the edges and seal well together. Cover with greased greaseproof paper or foil with a pleat in the centre and tie under the rim of the basin. Place in a saucepan filled with enough boiling water to come halfway up the sides of the basin. Cover and simmer for 2½ hours. Turn out on to a hot serving dish. To serve, make sure that everyone gets a bit of the lemon centre.

250 g (8 oz) self-raising flour
125 g (5 oz) shredded suet
150 ml (¼ pint) water

Filling:
125 g (4 oz) soft brown sugar
125 g (4 oz) mixed dried fruit
1 lemon
125 g (4 oz) unsalted butter

Serves 4–6
Preparation time: 15 minutes, plus chilling
Cooking time: 2½ hours

■ The 'pond' is the lemon and fruit mixture in the centre of the pudding. If liked, use any leftover suet pastry to make small swimmers. Cook balls of pastry for 20 minutes in boiling water; slit and fill with a little butter and brown sugar to serve.

treacle pudding

1 Butter a 900 ml (1½ pint) pudding basin. Then cream the butter or margarine and sugar together in a bowl until light and fluffy. Beat in the eggs, one at a time, adding a little of the flour with the second egg. Fold in the remaining flour.

2 Spoon 4 tablespoons of golden syrup into the buttered basin, then put the sponge mixture on top. Cover the basin with buttered foil, making a pleat across the centre to allow the pudding to rise. Stand the basin in a large saucepan with enough boiling water to come about halfway up the side of the basin. Boil steadily for 1½–2 hours, topping up with boiling water whenever necessary.

3 To make the sauce, heat the syrup and water in a small pan. Turn out the pudding on to a warmed serving dish and pour over the hot sauce just before serving.

125 g (4 oz) butter or margarine, plus extra for greasing

125 g (4 oz) caster sugar

2 large eggs

125 g (4 oz) self-raising flour, sifted

4 tablespoons golden syrup

Treacle Sauce:

4 tablespoons golden syrup

1 tablespoon water

Serves 4
Preparation time: 20–30 minutes
Cooking time: 1½–2 hours

■ To make a steamed jam sponge, use the jam of your choice in place of the golden syrup in both the bottom of the basin and in the sauce. Apricot and plum jam are particularly good.

index